Watermelon for ____

Written by Martha Rose Woodward

WINNER of Contest

Sponsored by Gourmand Magazine,

Madrid, Spain 2013

Special Award

BEST CookbooK in the World

About Watermelon

Dedication:

To my son, Barrett, for being there for me and for his tasty recipes.

ISBN-13: ISBN-13: 978-1466291171

ISBN-10: 1466291176 (CreateSpace-Assigned)

Children's book--non-fiction, watermelon for everyone, Watermelon for Everyone, watermelon, recipes, cookbook, watermelon salad, watermelon smoothie, watermelon recipes, watermelon jelly, watermelon chutney, gardening, food production, fruits, watermelon rind, Watermelon Promotion Board, watermelon festival in Cordele, GA, Watermelon Days Festival, watermelon growing, Butler Farm in Blount County, TN, watermelon spitting, watermelon history, watermelon lesson plans, Martha Rose Woodward, Knoxville's Sunsphere, Escape to Riches, Phillip Lim, Martha Woodward, Knoxville Journal Newspaper, Martha Sunsphere, Patricia Griffeth,

MarthaSunsphere.blogspot.com, Edouard Cointeau, Gourmand Magazine

Manufactured in the United States of America.

"Watermelon for Everyone" won an award from Gourmand Magazine in Madrid, Spain. Woodward became aware of the contest through an e mail dated 8/26/2013 written by Edouard Cointrea

Please send your book "Watermelon for Everyone," for the Gourmand Awards.

It is very special, and it might qualify for a Special Award.

The publication date is two years ago, but we have a special focus on watermelon this year.

Now I am in Beijing, for its BIBF Book Fair next week. I visited their huge Watermelon Museum. It is really well done. Your book should be there in Chinese.

Participating in our awards will give international exposure to your book.

You will find an entry form in the attached document,

Thank you.

Edouard Cointreau

E mail dated 8/27/2013, sent to Woodward from Edouard Cointreau

Thank you for sending your books.

After visiting the Watermelon Museum in Beijing – Daxing, I did an internet search on watermelon books around the world. I found your book.

You can find much information on internet and our web sites:
www.cookbookfair.com

www.gourmand-magazine.com

You can see hundreds of photos about us and our events on the website of our official photographer: www.tiborfoto.com

For the date, in a few special cases, we waive the date requirement. The jury made the rules, and can decide on exceptions.

Best Regards,

Edouard Cointreau

E mail from Gourmand Magazine to Ms. Woodward 12/21/2013

CONGRATULATIONS!!

E mail from Gourmand Magazine to Woodward 12/21/2013

CONGRATULATIONS!!

You receive this year a <u>SPECIAL AWARD OF THE JURY</u>

For your book: Watermelon for Everyone, Martha Rose Woodward, writer: Illustrations: Pat Griffeth. This is a very prestigious award.

You have already won and you will receive your Award on the stage at our next "Best in the World" event at Beijing Cookbook Fair on Tuesday May 20, 2014 if you do come.

In any case, please contact us as soon as possible .

For more information,conta

Edouard Cointreau, President

Gourmand World Cookbook Awards

Pintor Rosales, 50, 28008 Madrid-Spain

Watermelons are green-striped and oblong.

Watermelons are round and light green or dark green.

Some watermelons are small, weighing a pound or less.

Some watermelons are large and could weigh hundreds of pounds.

Most watermelons sold in stores weigh between five and fifteen pounds.

In Japan, farmers found a way to grow watermelons into a square shape.

The farmers use plastic containers to shape the melons as they grow on the vines.

Japanese farmers believe square melons are easier to stack on top of each other

when the melons are shipped to markets and stores all around the world.

In order to eat the flesh of a watermelon, burst it open and smell the fresh aroma of the jagged chunks.

This taste is like the first breathe of green grass on a cool Spring day.

Cut a watermelon with a knife. Hear it split like a zipper unzipping. Take a bite of the pure, seedless heart.

Feel the juice as it oozes over your chin. Taste the sweetness of the red pulp as it hits your tongue. Enjoy the natural treat that also happens to be good for you.

This is pure summer fun!

Butler
Farm

Blount
County,

Tennessee

Watermelon are sold in large grocery stores, at small stores along roads and highways and out of the backs of trucks.

They are sold almost everywhere.

Most melons are sold when whole, but many are cut into halves, fourths, or even into chunks and sold in serving sizes of cups or pints.

Watermelon is the second most popular fruit in the world.

How do watermelons grow?

Watermelon plants begin to grow when tiny seeds are planted in soil.

The seeds need sunshine, water and time to develop.

Soon the seeds change into small plants that push through the soil as they enter the world.

These plants continue to get larger and soon stretch out as long vines that produce yellow flowers that crawl across the ground. Each flower might become a melon.

Yellow flowers pop up along the watermelon vines. Bees, bats, birds, and butterflies pollinate the flowers when searching for the sweet nectar within the blooms. The animals get pollen, a sticky, yellow dust on their legs and carry the pollen from the daddy flower to the mother flower.

Each yellow flower that has been pollinated could germinate and produce a melon. As each pollinated flower closes up, a small bud of a melon appears. The bud continues to grow and develop until it matures into a full sized melon. Birds, bats, bees and butterflies love watermelon flowers.

Male flower

Female ovary

Both must be present or there will be no offspring.

Is watermelon a fruit or a vegetable?

Watermelon is a fruit because it is the ripened ovary and the contents of the ovary in a seed plant. Watermelon is most often thought of as a fruit because of its sweet flavor and sugar content.

Watermelon is a vegetable because a vegetable is defined as anything made or obtained from plants. Watermelon is a member of the curcurbitacae plant family of gourds.

(classified as Citrullus Lantus). Watermelon is related to gourds, cucumbers, squashes, and pumpkins.

Watermelon is grown in over half of the states in the USA. California, Florida, Texas, Arizona and Georgia grow the most in the USA, but many other states have huge watermelon crops.

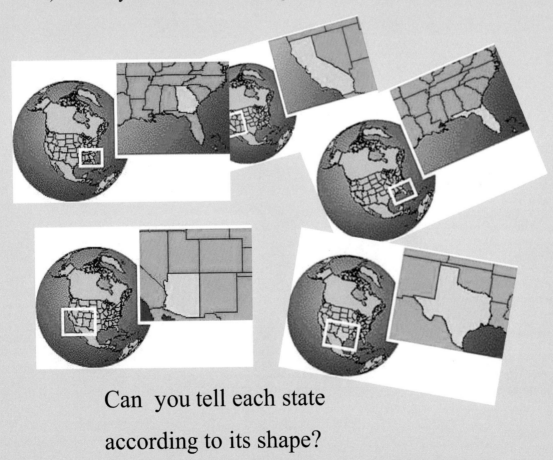

Can you tell each state

according to its shape?

Wally Melon is Cordele's mascot.

Cordele rhymes with bell.

The state of Georgia is known as the Watermelon Capital of the World. During the summer each year, the city of Cordele, Georgia celebrates the watermelon harvest with an annual Watermelon Days Festival. People come from all around the world to honor the red and green fruit.

The quality and quantities of watermelon grown in Cordele and the surrounding Crisp County are said to be some of the finest melons grown anywhere in the world.

Watermelons in China

The country of China is the number one producer of watermelons in the world with an estimated yearly production of over 69,000,000 metric tons. China needs that much watermelon in order to feed its population of over one billion people. Farmers enjoy growing watermelon and the sweet fruit is a popular choice for consumers.

No part of the watermelon goes to waste in China as the rind is often used in stir fry, stews or made into pickles. Watermelon juice is served as a beverage like orange juice and is also made into wine.

Watermelons also produce thousands of seeds. It is seen as shameful in China to spit seeds. Signs are posted in numerous places reminding consumers to never spit the seeds. Most people obey the rules.

Lim Lian Keng from Fukien, China

(1860-1918)

Lim Wah Mooi and Wee Hye Choo Neo

(married in China at age 16)

Watermelon in Africa

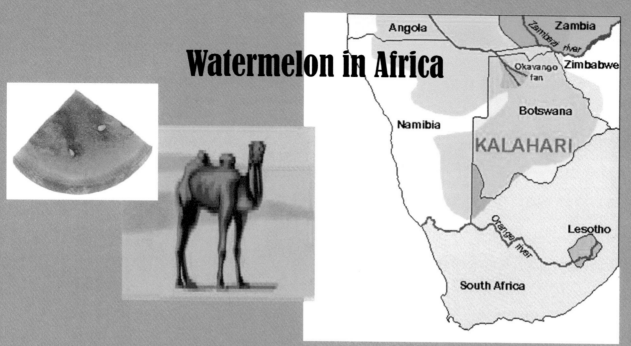

It is believed that watermelon plants first appeared in the Kalahari Desert thousands of years ago when the region received more rainfall. It is said that traveling merchants spread watermelons throughout the region by transporting the fruits and the plants on the backs of camels in caravans stretching for miles across the sands. Scientists also believe that the first watermelons contained flesh that was more clear or white than the pink-red-yellow melons seen today. White melons continue to be cultivated worldwide, but are rare.

Due to its high water content, its size and how it will keep, even in hot temperatures for many days, watermelon is well-suited for desert use.

The Kalahari Desert is located in southern Africa. It covers over 225,000 square miles and encompasses the countries of Angola, Zambia and Zimbabwe. The soil is made mostly of sand. It appears red, a dull brown or orange in color.

The name Kalahari is said to derive from the Tswana word Kgala, meaning "the great thirst" or Khalagari, Kgalagadi or Kalagare, meaning "a waterless place." Actually, the Kalahari is not defined as a true desert since it does receive approximately 9.8 inches of rainfall per year.

Geologists can tell from evidence in the sandy soil that the Kalahari Desert was once a much wetter place.

Watermelon in Japan

Farmers in the Zentsuji region of Japan developed a way to grow cubic watermelons. Square-shaped melons are easier to stack for shipment.

When the melons are small they are placed in glass or plastic, squared-shaped containers that look like boxes. As the melon gets larger it will naturally take the shape of the receptacle.

Pyramid-shaped and heart-shaped watermelons have also been grown.

The appeal to consumers is their novelty.

Square melons are expensive.

Thumping a Melon

To select a ripened melon, many people use the thumping method with great success.

Thumping means the melon is hit when a person flicks the middle finger off the thumb. (see photo)

This action should produce a deep, rich thudding sound on the melon. Melons that make a dull sound when thumped are not ripe or are overly ripe (too full of water) and should be avoided.

Directions for thumping a watermelon:

1. Place your thumb on top of your middle finger and press against your thumb nail bending your finger at the first joint.

2. This action should cause your finger and thumb to form a large O.

3. Move your middle finger so that it flips off your thumb.

4. Be sure your middle finger strikes the melon on the side.

5. Be sure you made a strong flick with your thumb.

6. If you hear a loud thump that sounds like a drum beat, you probably have a ripe melon. If you hear a thud or no clear sound, the melon is possibly too full of water or does not have enough water content.

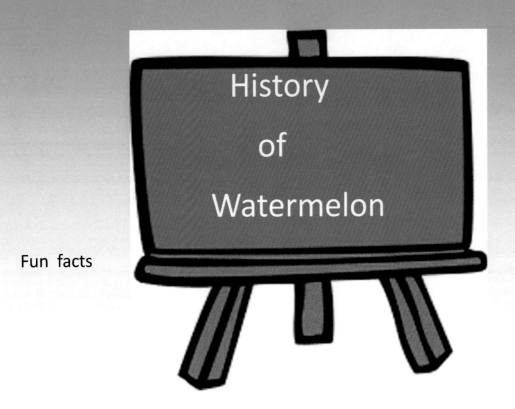

History of Watermelon

Fun facts

Early explorers used watermelons as canteens.

Watermelons were found in North America when the first European explorers arrived on the shores.

Native American Indians were highly skilled in the cultivation of watermelons.

Presidents George Washington and Thomas Jefferson grew watermelon in their gardens.

Early Greek settlers brought methods and recipes of pickling watermelon to South Carolina.

The first cookbook published in the United States in 1776 contained a recipe for pickles made from watermelon rind.

Watermelon is believed to have originated in the Kalahari Desert in Africa.

Melons seeds were found in burial tombs of Egyptians.

By the 9th Century, watermelons were seen in Europe, possibly spread along the Mediterranean Sea by way of merchant ships.

By the 10th Century, watermelons were seen in China.

By the 13th century watermelons were found in all parts of Europe and Asia.

More History of Watermelon with Fun Facts

A watermelon is 92% water.

There are over 1,200 varieties of watermelon.

The pulp or flesh of most watermelons is red, but other melons can be yellow, pink and even white.

The official scientific name of watermelon is Citrullus lanatus of the botanical family of Curcurbitacae.

Cucumbers, gourds, squashes and pumpkins are in the same botanical family as watermelons.

Watermelon is an excellent source of vitamins A,B6 and C.

A one cup serving of watermelon contains about 45 calories.

In inside part of the melon that has no seeds is known as the heart, the flesh is called pulp, and white fleshy part is rind and the covering is called skin.

A "Watermelon Slicing" is a social activity that became popular in the USA as far back as the 1600's.

During a Watermelon Slicing members of the community come together in a picnic-like setting to share melons. Each individual or family brings a melon to the event. The melons are sliced and spread out on long tables for everyone to sample. Watermelon Slicings are most often associated with schools, churches and political events.

Watermelon's flavor is enhanced with the flavors of pineapple, grapes, nuts, coconut and banana.

Watermelon Cookbook

The following pages contain recipes-both non-cooked and cooked- based on watermelon as the main ingredient. Watermelon is a special food in that it can be served as a sweet or as a savory dish. Watermelon pairs up very well with some other fruits, especially banana, pineapple, coconut, walnuts, pecans and peanuts and apples.

Non-cook recipes are a delightful way to teach children and students of all ages how to cook.

Recipes that require some cooking may also require special utensils and equipment.

BE SURE TO ADD SALT TO TASTE TO ALL RECIPES HAVING WATERMELON!

Quick and Easy Non-cook Recipes

Using

Watermelon

Watermelon Relish

Ingredients: 1 cucumber peeled and diced

2 cups watermelon; l/2 cup red onion (chopped); 2 tablespoons white distilled vinegar; 1 tablespoon chopped cilantro, salt to taste

Prepare cucumber, watermelon and onion.   Mix together; add vinegar and cilantro. Serve over crackers, pinto beans, chicken or hamburgers.

Watermelon Smoothie

Recipe can serve one or two people.

Ingredients: one or two cups fresh watermelon cut into chunks (remove seeds); l/2 cup to 3/4 cup vanilla ice cream or frozen yogurt; 2 to 4 ice cubes (use more if needed); 1 freshly peeled banana, chopped

  Place all ingredients into a blender or food processor and blend on medium speed.

Watermelon Icing

Ingredients: 1 cup light sour cream; 1 cup light whipped topping;

 1 cup powdered sugar; 1 to 2 cups fresh watermelon cut in chunks

Yields enough icing for a regular size, two layer cake.

Use white cake or red velvet cake mix when making the cake.

Add all ingredients to a large mixing bowl and sire. Mix thoroughly. Spread onto cake or use on cupcakes. Use fresh melon balls as garnish.

Be sure to drain the water from the melon or the icing will be too run-ny.

Watermelon Fruit Salad

 Ingredients: 2 cups chunky pineapple; 1 fresh apple peeled and cored; 2 cups fresh watermelon made into balls, cubes or chunks; 1 sliced

banana; 1 cup grapes; 1/4 cup chopped fresh cilantro; 1/2 cup pecans

Salt, if needed.

 Mix all ingredients in large bowl . Serve over ice cream or yogurt.

Barrett's Greek Salad with Watermelon

Ingredients:

1 red onion the size of a tennis ball, peeled and sliced into rings; 1 tomato the size of your fist, peeled and chopped in chunks ; ½ cucumber peeled and chopped into chunks; l/2 cup feta cheese, broken into small bites; 2 tablespoons olive oil 1/2 cup black olives chopped; 1 to 2 cups fresh watermelon, chopped into chunks (Be sure the take the seeds out.) Salt to taste.

Directions:

Prepare the vegetables and watermelon; add to large mixing bowl. Drizzle olive oil on top. Stir thoroughly. Add feta cheese. Place in frig for up to one hour or serve immediately.

7 Cup Watermelon Fruit Salad

Ingredients: 2 cups chunks watermelon with seeds removed; 1 cup sliced banana; 1 cup pineapple chunks; 1 cup orange chunks; 1 cup seedless grapes; l/2 cup nuts; and l/2 cup coconut flakes

Place in large mixing bowl and stir thoroughly.

Variation of the 7 Cup Watermelon Fruit Salad –11 Cup

Make the above salad as directed. Add: 1 cup sour cream; 2 cups whipped topping; and 1 cup confectioner's sugar. (Use reduced fat and reduced calorie options if desired). Mix and store in refrigerator until ready to be eaten.

Watermelon Lemonade

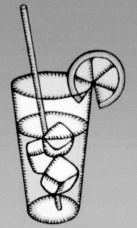

This recipe yields one serving:

Ingredients: one cup fresh watermelon cut into cubes, chunks or small pieces; 8 ounces lemon juice (fresh or frozen concentrate) 6 to 8 ice cubes; sugar-if desired.

Directions: Place one cup of watermelon into blender along with 8 ounces of lemonade. Add 6 to 8 ice cubes and blend until smooth.

Melon Balls

Ingredients: Fresh watermelon

Directions: Make melon balls using a fruit scoop or melon ball maker. A large melon will produce hundreds of 3/4 ounce melon balls. Be sure to keep melon balls cold until served. Use in salads or to top desserts. Freeze and use as ice cubes in drinks.

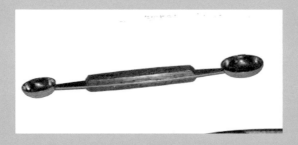

Melon ball maker

Watermelon Ice Cubes

You will need a blender or food processor.

Ingredients:

2 to 4 cups of fresh watermelon, cut into chunks

Ice trays and a freezer

Directions: Place watermelon in blender or food processor and

blend until smooth. Pour mixture into ice trays and place in freezer

and freeze.. Serve in lemonade, sodas, or just eat the cubes.

Barrett's Modified Apple Salad with Watermelon

Ingredients:

1 cup red or green seedless grapes ; 1 fresh apple, cored and chopped into chunks, salt to taste

l/2 cup walnuts (Use pecans if you prefer) ; 1 cup celery finely chopped

2 cups chopped watermelon (Be sure to remove the seeds and drain all liquid);

¾ cup mayonnaise: l//2 tablespoon lemon juice (save until last) ;, leaf lettuce, if desired

Directions: Prepare ingredients by chopping and measuring.

Add to large mixing bowl and stir thoroughly.

Drizzle lemon juice on top.

Serve on top of leaf lettuce, if desired.

Watermelon and Yogurt Parfait

Ingredients: (serves 1 or 2 persons)

  1 cup plain yogurt OR whipped topping OR vanilla ice cream

  1/2 cup watermelon chunks (drain water)

  1 T. raisins OR 8 to 10 fresh grapes

  1 T coconut flakes

  1 or 2 T. granola or chopped pecans, OR peanuts OR walnuts

Directions: Mix all ingredients in a tall glass or parfait container, start with the yogurt and rotate ingredients, ending with watermelon on top; serve immediately. To make this recipe for more than one person, double or triple as needed.

Watermelon and Cream Cheese Bagel

Ingredients: 1 bagel-plain; 8 to 10 watermelon chunks; 2 T. cream cheese, salt.

Directions: Cut bagel in half. Mix watermelon and cream cheese together and spread onto bread.

Martha's Alternating Bean Watermelon Salad

Ingredients: 1 can (16 oz.) pinto beans OR black beans OR white beans; 1 cup watermelon chunks (drained); 1/2 cup chopped red onion; 1/2 cup chopped green pepper; 1 small tomato chopped (about 1/2 cup); jalapeno pepper to taste; 1 T. cilantro; 1 T fresh parsley; salt and pepper. Add 1/2 cup whole kernel corn, if desired. Salt to taste.

Directions: Mix all ingredients in your serving dish; be sure to stir thoroughly. (This dish keeps well if refrigerated).

Watermelon Chutney

Chutney is said to have originated in India. It is basically a mixture of fruit, vinegar, sugar, herbs and spices. It was probably developed as a way to preserve fruits that possibly had a high rate of spoilage. Chutney is generally a thick mixture having large chunks of the fruit and other ingredients. It is often used as a sauce or topping.

Ingredients

To make about one pint of chutney, you will need:

4 cups watermelon, drain the juice, 1/2 medium sized, red onion, chopped

 2 tablespoons apple cider vinegar, 2 tablespoons nuts of your choice (pecans or walnuts; can also use peanuts)

1 1/2 cups (light) brown sugar, 1 tablespoon minced garlic

1 tablespoon minced ginger , 1/4 teaspoon cloves, ground

1 teaspoon grated lemon zest, Juice squeezed from 1 lemon or l tablespoon lemon juice from jar, salt to taste.

(If you prefer to add heat to this dish, add l/4 teaspoon red chili pepper flakes or l/2 cut fresh jalapeno pepper or sprinkle on red hot chili sauce to taste.)

Salt to taste

Instructions: Place watermelon in blender or food processor and mix until chunks are lumpy. Place this mixture in saucepan and bring to a rolling boil. Simmer watermelon over medium heat until it is reduced to about 2 cups. Combine all ingredients, add to juice and simmer until almost dry. Chill and serve.

Watermelon Rind Pickles

Ingredients: 1 watermelon 10-12 pound. You are only going to use the rind.*
6 cups water (more for rinsing) 1/3 cup pickling salt ; 3 1/2 cups white granulated sugar ; 1 1/2 cups white vinegar ; 5 or 6 sticks of cinnamon (Some people use "red hot" cinnamon candy and this seems to work well.) ; 2 teaspoons whole cloves
*rind: white section of melon between the skin and the red/pink/or yellow pulp
You will have to use more water for rinsing and boiling; amounts will vary.

Supplies: a colander and a sieve; large cook pot-4 to 6 quart size, a stove or stove top, 6- l/2 pint-size canning jars; large canning pot, tongs

Directions: Cut rind from watermelon that has red/pink/yellow flesh and hard outer skin removed. This will make about 9 cups. Cut the rind into 1 inch squares or other 1 inch shapes. Place 9 cups rind in a large nonmetal bowl and combine the 6 cups water and pickling salt; pour salt and water mixture over rind, add more to make certain all portions of the rind are covered. Cover bowl and allow to stay at room temperature overnight. (This is the pickling process). Place a colander in the sink and pour the rind mixture into it; let water drain. (You do not need to save the salt water mixture). Rinse mixture under cold water; drain well. Transfer rind to a large pot; four quart size is recommend. Add enough cold water to cover rind. Bring to a rolling boil; reduce heat. Simmer while pot is covered for 20 to 25 minutes or until rind is tender or can be easily poked through with a fork; drain. To make syrup, using a 6 to 8 quart stainless steel, enamel, or nonstick pot, combine sugar, vinegar, the 1 1/2 cups water, the cinnamon sticks, and cloves. Bring to a rolling boil stirring until sugar dissolves; reduce heat. Simmer, uncovered for 10 minutes and be sure to stir. Strain mixture through a sieve and KEEP THE LIQUID. Remove cloves and cinnamon stick. Return liquid to the same cook pot you were using. Add watermelon rind to syrup mixture in the pot. Bring to rolling boil; reduce heat. Simmer, covered for 25 to 30 minutes or until rind is translucent. The liquid should be thickened. Remove from heat. Spoon hot rind and syrup into sterilized half pint canning jars, leaving 1/2 inch at the top of each jar. Be sure there is no liquid on the rims. Place lids on jars and adjust to fit tightly. Place jars in a boiling water canner for 10 minutes at a full boil. Remove jars and place on counter to cool. This recipe should make 6 half pint jars. As jars cool you should hear a popping sound. This means the jars are sealed.

Watermelon Juice Jelly

Before you begin, if you have never made jelly before there are specific kitchen tools you will need you probably do not yet own. Utensils needed: large, stainless-steel cook pot; large canning pot (one that holds about 8 to 10 glass jars), tongs, new lids, rubber sealers and rings, a sieve, a colander and jelly has to be boiled on top of the stove.

Ingredients: 6 cups watermelon juice; 2 cups sugar ; 4 T. bottled lemon juice; Pectin-usually takes a small box ; 6 half pint jars or 8 to 10 cup jars

Directions: Make watermelon juice by pressing the watermelon pulp through a fine mesh strainer or use a blender to cream the chunks of melon first and strain through the mesh strainer afterward. (You may decide to choose to leave the juice rather thick containing pulp. This is okay, but the jelly will look more like jam than a clear product.)

In a 6 to 8 quart stainless-steel pot, combine the watermelon juice, sugar and lemon juice. Bring the mixture to a full rolling boil over high heat, stirring constantly for 2 to 4 minutes. Stir in the pectin gently, add it carefully, being sure it does not clump. Return mixture to a full rolling boil, boil hard for 1 minute, stirring constantly with a wire whisk to avoid clumping of the pectin. Take off heat. Skim off foam. Check the consistency of this mixture. It should look and feel like jelly at this point. As it cools it will firm up even more.

Ladle the jelly into sterilized jars leaving 1/4" space at the top of each jar. Be sure each jar has been washed clean and it is a good idea to boil the jars before you make jelly. Wipe away all drips. Use new lids, seals and rings and seal each jar fairly tight, but do not go overboard. Place the jars into a water bath canner and process in boiling water for 10 minutes.

Makes 6 half-pints, or will possibly fill 8 to 10 cup jars. Place the jars on a counter or table and listen for the sound of a pop; this means the lid is sealing. If you **do not hear the pop, your jelly may need to be eaten soon as it possibly won't store well for a long period of time.**

Watermelon rind

It is environmentally savvy to use watermelon rind.

Barrett's Last Minute Chicken with Water-melon

Ingredients: chicken breasts (1 per person to be served)

Fresh corn cut from cob (1 cob per person served); Watermelon (1/2 cup chunks per piece chicken, 1 T cilantro, red onion-sliced into rings (5 to 8 uncooked rings); Jalapeno pepper to taste or no pepper; Salt and pepper to taste; Grill or prepare children in a pan until cooked like you prefer.; Remove corn from cob and heat in frying pan until cooked.; Chop cilantro and jalapeno; add the amount of watermelon to suit your taste. Salt and pepper to taste.

Watermelon Cobbler Pie

Ingredients: 2 cups watermelon; 1 cup sugar; l/2 stick butter, pinch vanilla flavoring; biscuit dough

You can make biscuits from scratch or use a canned product. If you are making biscuits, use the recipe on the biscuit mix you purchase or a recipe from a book.

Directions: Place watermelon and sugar in a mixing bowl, mix thoroughly-be sure the watermelon is covered with the sugar, cut butter into small pieces and toss on top of mixture; add pinch of flavoring. Take biscuit dough and break into bite-size pieces, toss these on top of watermelon mixture. Add up to 2 tablespoons water. Salt to taste. Be sure to ONLY add a small amount of vanilla flavoring; it can take over this dish. (l/16 of teaspoon-=inch)

Bake in 350 degree over for 25 to 35 minutes. Should be done when biscuits are golden brown and mixture is bubbling. Serve with ice cream or frozen yogurt.

Lesson Plans Using Watermelons

Lesson Plan #1

Math-Problem solving; estimation

Time needed: 45 minutes to 1 hour   Grade levels: K through college

This lesson involves several steps and can be modified for an entire class or used with small groups of students of all ages. An entire class can complete the lesson with one melon or small groups of 3 to 6 students can use a melon each.

Objectives: The student will use the math skills of problem solving, addition, estimation, subtraction, fractions, drawing conclusions, predicting outcomes, finding mean, median, and mode, determining the weight of an object in pounds and ounces using scales, recording data on charts, larger than/less than, and writing questions.

Materials needed: One whole watermelon or one melon per group of students, paper/pencil/markers, charts, scales, towels, plastic knives, napkins

Directions: Ask students what it means to guess. Introduce the word "estimation" and give the meaning as guessing. Give each student a small piece of paper and ask them to write his/her name on the paper. Next, show the melon and ask each student to write his/her guess as to how much the melon weighs on the paper. Take the papers up and write their guesses beside their names on a large chart or on a display board. Ask who made the largest guess? The smallest?

Lesson Plans Using Watermelons

Lesson Plan #1 (continued)

Math-Problem solving; estimation

Have the students to add the total for all guesses; find the average. Teach the concepts of mean; median and mode.

Weigh the melon. Check to see if anyone guess the exact weight. Let the students tell you who made the closest guess and whose was the least closest.

Ask the students to ask some questions about the estimation of the weight of a melon. Did most students guess nearest to the correct weight? Do melons weigh less or more than they look like they could? Ask the students how many parts you have if you cut the melon into half? Cut the melon and keep asking about fractional parts.

End the lesson by letting the class eat the watermelon.

Lesson #2

Fractions--halves/ fourths/eighths

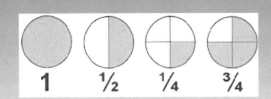

Objectives: The students will use watermelon to explore math and reading skills.

Students will read directions, determine sequence, determine cause and effect, discuss the results of an activity, and produce original art work.

In order for students to learn the most from Lesson #2, they need to complete Lesson #1. first.

Materials needed: A watermelon (WITH SEEDS) for the entire class or one per group of 3 to 6 students. Towels and napkins. Paper/pencil/markers/crayons. Class charts and board space.

Directions: Using one whole watermelon, the teacher will ask the students to predict how many pieces will result if she/he cuts the melon one time in equal parts. The teacher writes 1/2 on the board and also 2/2 while discussing. Next, ask how many pieces result when the 1/2 sections are cut into equal parts. ¼ + ¼ . Also write ¾ and 4/4 on the board.

Ask the students to copy and solve ¼ + 2/4 +   ¼+ ¾ = and 2/4 + 2/4= ½+½=

Continue with fourths and eighths until all have mastered these skills.

Ask the students to divide the melon that has been cut into equal parts so that each class member gets an equal share. Students may need to cut some pieces to different sizes.

Ask the students how many parts you have if you cut the melon into half? Cut the melon and keep asking about fractional parts. You may also teach adding fractions if you have time.

Lesson Plan #3

Artwork using fresh melon and seeds.

Skills: addition, mean, median, mode

Give each student a piece of melon. Ask them estimate how many seeds they think are in their piece of melon and to write it on paper. Next, tell them to count the number of seeds in their piece of melon and write the total.

Ask each student to share their total with a partner or group of other students. Ask the students to add their totals. Keep going until all are added and there is a class total.

Find the class total, the average, and mean and the mode. Check to see if anyone guess correctly. Determine who got the closest, etc.

Students may eat the melon, but tell them to save the seeds.

Ask students to create a colorful piece of artwork using seeds, crayons, and/or pencil drawings.

Ask students to share their artwork and to discuss their inspiration; others may ask questions. Use artwork to decorate the classroom.

Watermelon IQ Quiz

How much do you know about watermelon?

Answer the following questions.

(Answer Key found on Bibliography page)

1. A watermelon can weigh:

A. 800 to 900 pounds B. 1 to 262 pounds C. to 3/4 ounces

2. Watermelon is what percentage water?

   A. 100% B. 50% C. 92%

3. Watermelon is believed to have originated in what desert?

A. Sahara B. Kalahari C. Death Valley

4. Watermelon can be what colors?

A. Red, pink, yellow, white

B. Blue and purple

C. brown and orange

5. What vitamins are in watermelon?

A. Vitamin C B. Vitamins A, B6 and C. None

6. What food is watermelon most like? A. lettuce B. kale C. cucumber

7. How many calories are in one cup of watermelon? A. 45 B. 25 C. 100

8. What animals pollinate watermelon flowers? A. bees, bats, birds, butter-flies B. raccoons and squirrels   C. lizards and snakes

9. Thumping a melon means you? A. dig it up B. strike it with your finger C. eat it

10. Name the shapes a watermelon might be?

A. round or oblong B. square, triangular, round, oblong C. both A and B

About the author

Martha Rose Woodward is a retired school teacher who developed her interests in writing, journalism, and television and radio production after she left the field of education in 1999 after 24 years in the classroom due to a serious health issue. She began writing in 2007 and has published more than 1,000 articles for the Knoxville Journal Newspaper since that time. She lives in an historic Victorian home in Knoxville, Tennessee and spends her free time with her three grown children, Barrett, Erin and Ashley Rose. She also enjoys the family's three dogs and 8 ducks. Woodward is an avid quilt maker, videographer, gardener and seamstress.

Other books by Martha Rose Woodward:

Knoxville's Sunsphere; Biography of a Landmark 2007

Knoxville's 1982 World's Fair-2009

Seven Minutes in Hell: The Eric McLean Murder Case 2009

Even Wounded Birds Fly--a novel 2008

Watermelon for Everyone--a children's book 2011

1982 World's Fair-Revised 2012 edition

No Spitting Watermelon Seeds-a children's book 2012

Escape to Riches 2012

Watermelon for Everyone-Revised 2013 History -Recipes-Lesson Plans

Martha and Patricia 2011

Something Spook at the Sunsphere-2013

About the Illustrator

Patricia Griffeth is a graphic designer who has worked on many magazines and publications. She has been in the publishing and printing industry her entire life. Currently, she works at the Knoxville Journal Newspaper as Production Editor and Graphic Designer. She has contributed to many other books, but this is her first children's book. She was selected to work on this book due to her work ethic and skills as an artist. She has long dreamed of illustrating a children's book. She has hoped to inspire her grandchildren to have a love for reading and has read to them every night they spend at her home. She also volunteered at their school as a reading volunteer. She said that working on this book has been fun and she is pleased with the results. She will definitely search for other opportunities to illustrate more books.

Bibliography

The Butler Farm in Blount County, TN

http://www.cordelecrispga.com

http://www.giantwatermelons.com

http://www.nationalwatermelonassociation.com

www.ncmelons.com/

http://ohioline.osu.edu/h' -fact/1000/1626.html

Publisher Software supplied all clip

http://www.watermelon.org/

Watermelon Days Festival , Cordele, Georg

Wikipedia entries for watermelon

ANSWER KEY TO IQ QUIZ: I. B 2. C 3. B 4. A 5. B 6. C 7. A 8. A 9. B 10. C

Much of the information for this book was used with permission from the: Nati
Watermelon Promotion Board, 3361 Rouse Road, Suite 150,   Orlando, FL 32

Recipes supplied by Barrett Buie, Knoxville, Tennes

On-line Reviews

Best Books About Watermelons for Classroom Use

Killeen Gonzalez, Yahoo! Contributor Network
Feb 4, 2013 "Share your voice on Yahoo! websites.

Are you planning on incorporating watermelons into your Pre-K student's lesson
plans? Have you already selected a handful of stories to go with the unit? If not, you
may want to consider using one of the following books:

"Watermelon for Everyone"

If you ask me, Martha Rose Woodward's book "Watermelon for Everyone" would be
perfect as an introduction to a science unit. It would also pair well with Julie Murray's
"Watermelon Life Cycles." Both focus on how a watermelon grows.

2013: Watermelon for Everyone-Revised edition has been nominated for the Gourmand World Cookbook Award in Madrid, Spain in August 2013.

MANY THANKS TO PHILLIP LIM FOR THE USE OF HISTORIC PHOTOS OF HIS
RELATIVES FROM CHINA

Another book about watermelon written by Martha Rose Woodward

"No Spitting Watermelon Seeds."

Each page in this book contains rhymes and repetition of one special line. Everyone enjoys the reminders that it is not polite to spit watermelon seeds. But, there is a fun ending.

Eva Whitson is the child model used on this cover.

Made in the USA
San Bernardino, CA
23 July 2018